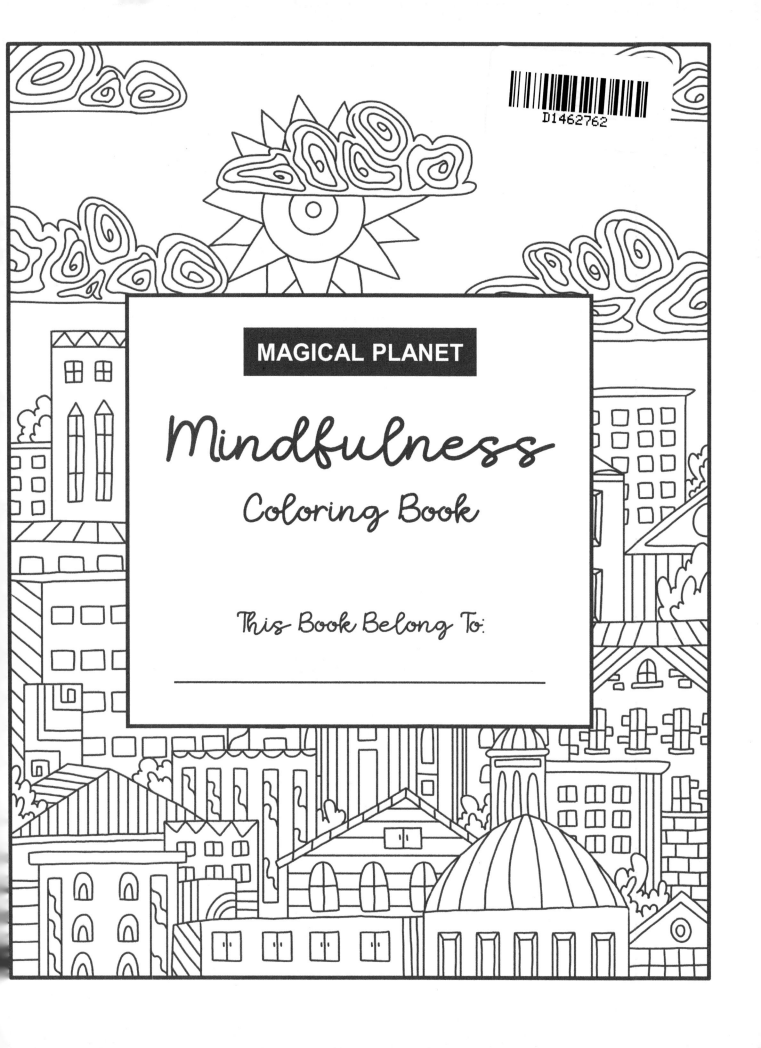

MAGICAL PLANET

Mindfulness
Coloring Book

This Book Belong To:

_____

Hello Coloring Friends!

Thank you for purchasing this book. We appreciate your support, We sincerely hope that you find enjoyment and contentment in these pages! Happy coloring!

Tips For Coloring

This paper is best suited for colored pencils, gel pens and markers. For all illustrations, it's separately printed sheets to prevent bleed-through and allow you to easily remove and frame your favorite artwork!

Please Share Your Experience On Amazon

We hope you have a memorable coloring journey with this book, and we'd love to receive your feedback, which helps us improve and continuously provides great products, also helps others like you to find us and make confident decisions.

We have a freebie for you!

Scan the **QR Code**
To get news, offers & free pages

Copyright © 2022 Magical Planet

About Magical Planet:

Magical Planet is a family-run publishing business! Passionate about creating beautiful original detailed illustrations for children, teens, and adults, we believe that art and color are genuine gifts to the world. It is a tool that transcends cultural, age, gender, and ethnic boundaries, allowing everyone to explore themselves and their surroundings, and when it comes to coloring, there is no mistake, only unique creations.

Unleash your inner artist and make your masterpiece with this coloring book, forget all the worries of the moment and enjoy these coloring pages on your own **Magical Planet**, these coloring pages will heal your soul and release your stress.

Magic Is Something You Make, **Stay Magical!** ★

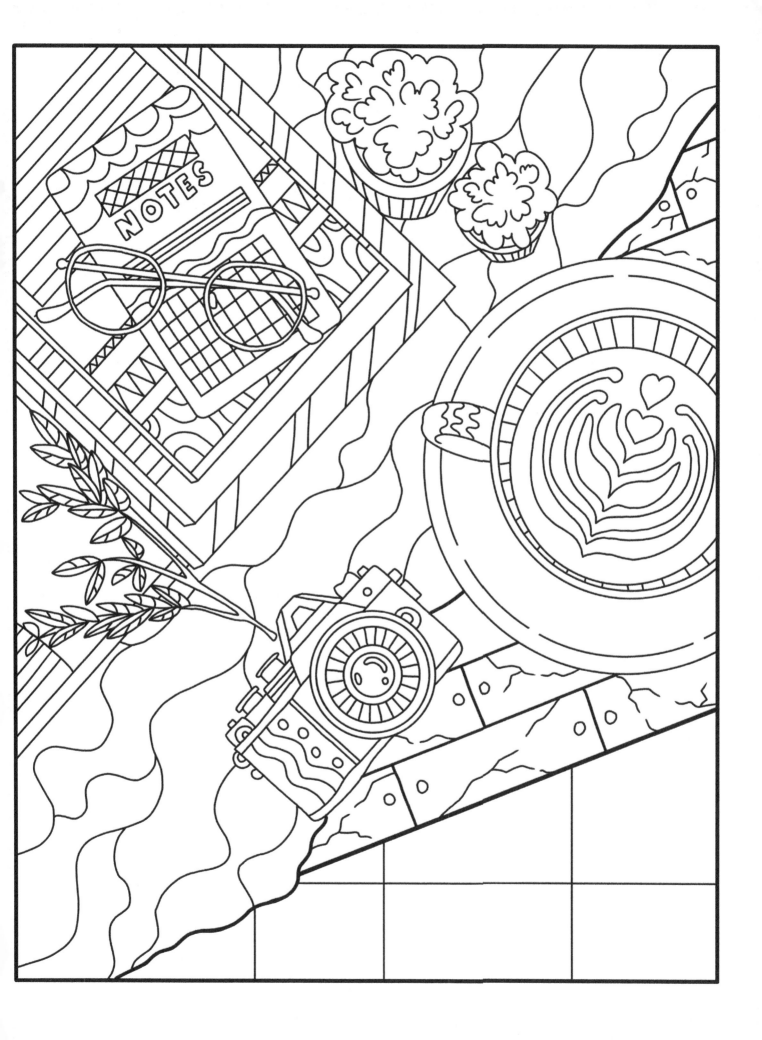

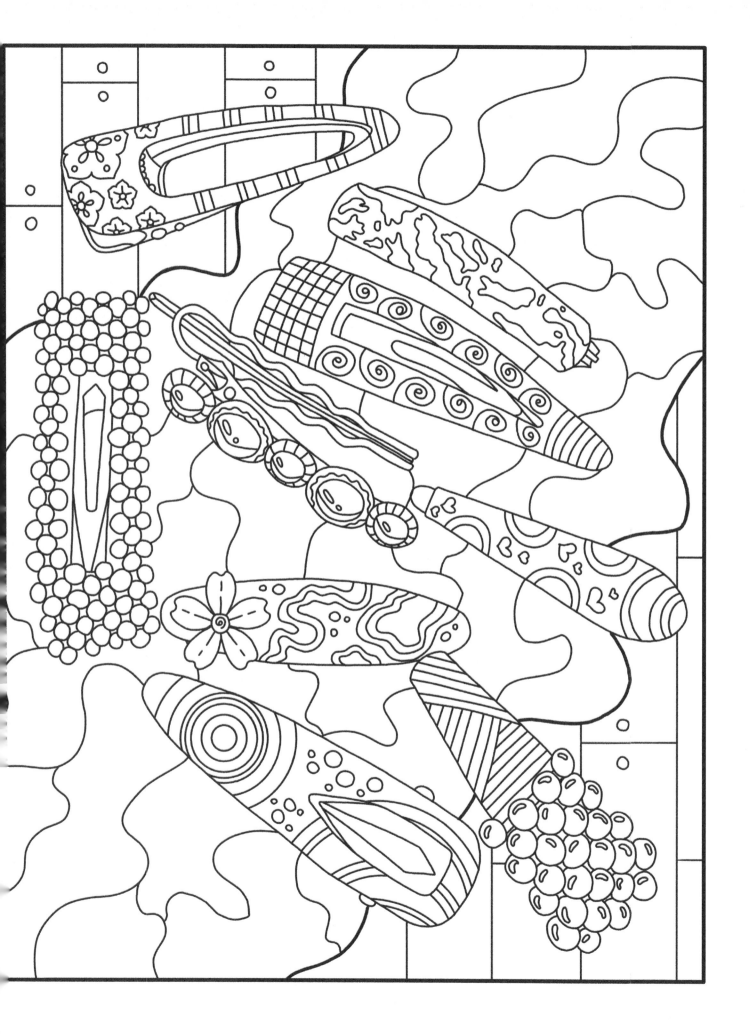

Made in the USA
Monee, IL
13 December 2022

21408238R00044